Candles

John Bird and Dorothy Diamond

A Chelsea College Project sponsored by the Nuffield Foundation and the Social Science Research Council

Published for Chelsea College, University of London, by Macdonald Educational, London and Milwaukee

Published by
Macdonald & Co (Publishers) Ltd
Maxwell House
Worship Street
London EC2A 2EN

First published in 1975
Reprinted 1983

ISBN 0 356 05070 X

Library of Congress Catalog Card Number
77-82987

Project team

Project organizer : John Bird

Team members :   Dorothy Diamond (full-time)
                 Keith Geary
                 Don Plimmer
                 Ed Catherall

Evaluators :   Ted Johnstone
                 Tom Robertson

Editors

Penny Butler
Macdonald Educational

John Pettit
Nuffield Foundation Science Teaching Project
Publications Department

Made and printed by Chorley & Pickersgill Limited, Leeds

General preface

The books published under the series title Teaching Primary Science are the work of the College Curriculum Science Studies project. This project is sponsored jointly by the Nuffield Foundation and the Social Science Research Council. It aims to provide support and guidance to students who are about to teach science in primary schools.

Although the College Curriculum Science Studies materials have been produced with the student teacher very much in mind, we suggest that they will also be of use to teachers and to lecturers or advisers—in fact to anyone with an interest in primary school science. Hence this series of books.

Three main questions are considered important:

What is science?

Why teach science?

How does one teach science?

A very broad view is taken of teacher training. Training does not, and should not, stop once an in-service or college course has been completed, but can and does take place on a self-help basis in the classroom. In each context, however, we consider that it works best through the combined effects of:

1 Science Science activities studied practically at the teacher's level before use in class.

2 Children Observation of children's scientific activities and their responses to particular methods of teaching and class organization.

3 Teachers Consideration of the methods used by colleagues in the classroom.

4 Resources A study of materials useful in the teaching of science.

5 Discussion and thought A critical consideration of the *what*, the *why* and the *how* of science teaching, on the basis of these experiences. This is particularly important because we feel that there is no one way of teaching any more than there is any one totally satisfactory solution to a scientific problem. It is a question of the individual teacher having to make the 'best' choice available to him in a particular situation.

To help with this choice there are, at frequent intervals, special points to consider; these are marked by a coloured tint. We hope that they will stimulate answers to such questions as 'How did this teacher approach a teaching problem? Did it work for him? Would it work for me? What have I done in a situation like that?' In this way the reader can look critically at his own experience and share it by discussion with colleagues.

All our books reflect this five-fold pattern of experiences, although there are differences of emphasis. For example, some lay more stress on particular science topics and others on teaching methods.

In addition, there is a lecturers' guide *Students, teachers and science* which deals specifically with different methods and approaches suitable for the college or in-service course in primary science but, like the other books in the series, it should be of use to students and teachers as well as to lecturers.

Contents

Introduction

In 1860 Michael Faraday gave a series of lectures at the Royal Institution in London on 'The Chemical History of the Candle'. These lectures proved to be a landmark in the history of popular education because they gave a striking illustration of how much science can come from the study of the simplest everyday objects. Since Faraday's time the candle has become much less 'everyday', although birthdays, Christmas and power cuts ensure that it still has a place in the home. But it has lost none of its power to attract the curiosity and excitement of many children nor, for that matter, of adults. The candle has been a frequent topic in books on primary science, and figures in the recent primary science projects such as Schools Council Science 5/13 and Nuffield Junior Science.

This book illustrates something of the scientific potential of the candle which Faraday demonstrated so elegantly in his lectures. A selection of the many investigations for which the candle is a starting point is described. As well as giving ideas for classroom work, this is used to give some idea of *what* science is.

Despite its importance, the reason *why* we should teach science is rarely considered. Some possible reasons are advanced, using some of these investigations as illustrated examples.

When we come to consider *how* to use the candle in the classroom, certain advantages and problems immediately become apparent. One advantage is that candles are relatively cheap and easy to use ; the one major problem is that of safety.

As in the home, some of the most worthwhile activities involve an element of risk—but sensible precautions and adequate supervision reduce it to negligible proportions, provided that the teacher knows beforehand the nature and the magnitude of the dangers, and always errs on the side of caution. For this reason special emphasis is given to the possible safety problems and how to overcome them. Different methods of grouping and organization are also suggested, providing a graded range of choices so that a teacher can select whichever method will maintain an adequate level of control and safety in the classroom.

These precautions, combined at appropriate moments with discussion, will not only produce a safe classroom environment but also safety-conscious children.

See bibliography : 4.

My candle

The main part of the candle is the wax with a wick through the centre.

As the flame grows more of the wick shows and the wax melts, the wax melts from the heat of the flame.

The flame is not bright all over it is dark near the ~~the~~ wick.

It is at its brightest at the top.

There is yellow at the top of the flame and grey and at the bottom and blue near the wick.

I can read newsprint through the flame at the bottom by the wick.

The flame is a cone shape

The flame is pointed at the top

1 Deciding what to do

What aspects of science will you develop in class through this topic? The first problem is simply one of getting enough ideas. These will be thought out in a relatively leisurely fashion when you are planning class work, or more urgently in response to a child's question or a restive class.

In one or both cases useful ideas will come, not only directly from the teacher, but by:

Discussion with the children.
A search for more detailed information in books and other sources.

There are many detailed suggestions in the text. You are also referred to Chapter 9 and the bibliography, which should be of special assistance in planning.

Factors influencing choice

Once you have sufficient ideas you will need to decide which to include or exclude. Your choice may depend on:

Interest   You will need to ask yourself: 'Is each of these ideas likely to interest the children?' If an idea has come from *them* it is likely that this is so. If not, care should be taken to discuss all the possibilities with them first, and to give at least some opportunity for modification and choice.

Ability   Will the children have the knowledge or skill to carry out the activities successfully?

Organization   For example, do problems like cost or safety present difficulties? (See Chapter 2.)

Aims and objectives   What is the value of this activity to children? Is it because, for example:

It's fun?

It will help develop skills like observation, explanation, or experiment (Chapters 3, 4, 5 and 6)?

It will build up knowledge of ideas like melting or burning?

A more detailed list of aims and objectives can be found in the back of any Schools Council Science 5/13 book. Part of this list is given on page 20 of this book.

2 Problems of organization

Basic materials

You will need some common types of candle:

Birthday cake candles
Household candles (or half candles)
Nightlights
Tapers (or half tapers)

You may want to use all, or some, of these types, but if it is a question of *choice* some important factors are:

Safety Beware particularly of the danger of the candle toppling over.

Cost Which of these types costs the most, and which the least?

Ease of observation Which type produces the most dramatic and easily observed flame?

Setting up the candle

This needs some practice and experiment beforehand.
Many activities suggested use the single candle fixed in a suitable container, so it is important to work out a method that is safe and avoids mess and damage to furniture. Try:

The taper or birthday candle with its base fixed in a lump of Plasticine.
The candle in a yoghurt carton of damp sand.
The nightlight or half candle in a tin of damp sand.
Newspaper and/or asbestos sheet as a protection for the table surface.
Damp sand, or newspaper, to put out any small fires.

Caution Expanded polystyrene ceiling tiles might be suggested as a base for a candle. These should never be used, as this material is inflammable.

Which materials and methods do you find the most satisfactory? See bibliography: 4.

The mechanics of class organization

Whatever general kind of activity is going on in the classroom, the candle securely set up in its container is likely to be used in *either* or *both* of the following ways:

1 Teacher-controlled 'demonstration' The teacher sets up activities and discusses these with a group or class of children. Here the teacher has complete control of the materials. *For safety reasons this is the best way in which this topic can be used with nursery and infant children*, but it is a method which need by no means be restricted to this age group.

Provided the activities are linked to children's interests— for example, in birthday cake candles—and provided the children are encouraged to talk, this method can result in much useful and enjoyable scientific discussion.

One of the main problems here is ensuring the children can see clearly what is going on.

What advantages and/or problems do you find from the use of this method?

2 Group work by the children This can be done more or less independently, in one or more small groups.

There are two main possibilities here: either the children will sit or stand *round* a group of tables or desk units, or *face* a table or a fixed bench at the *side* of the classroom. In either case it is important to:

Avoid overcrowding and ensure ease of observation.
Ensure that the candle is positioned safely.

Here is an example; how does it illustrate the points made above?

Beginning

Assuming that you will have at least some group work going on, how will you make a start? You may need to decide the following issues.

Starting points Should you fit the candle topic into a general integrated class theme, or do you wish it to be distinct from other activities?

What activities will you start the children on and how might these develop? The succeeding chapters, in particular Chapter 9, will give you some ideas.

Grouping How many groups will be involved? How large will each group be, bearing in mind the nature of the activity and the availability of books and materials?

Are there some points at which each child in the class might be involved in a particular activity, for example creative writing?

Materials Have you sufficient materials? Have you sufficient spares? Will any materials need to be bought?

Position Where should the groups be placed? Bear in mind, in particular, the need for:

Easy access to resources and services.
Avoidance of unnecessary traffic through the classroom.
Class supervision (where safety is involved).

Furniture Is it necessary to reorganize classroom furniture? If so, how?

Speed and sequence Should some activities logically follow others? Will some activities be finished more quickly than others? In this case, what will the children do when they are finished?

What will the rest do? If only some of the class are involved, what will the others be doing at the same time?

It is important to avoid over-committing yourself.

Communication What methods might you use?

Talk with the class, a group, or an individual?
Use of the blackboard, or workcards?
Use of class displays?

What special purposes might each method serve? Consider the uses and limitations of each for:

Giving instructions about organization.
Giving information.
Getting children's ideas.
Clarifying understanding.
Stimulating interest.

Use these and, possibly, other points to consider critically the following examples.

Teacher *A*, with a class of thirty children aged between ten and eleven, has discussed a class project based on the theme 'fire'. They have visited a local fire station.

After some discussion with the children the following ideas are decided upon:

Ways in which fire is useful to man.
A study of fire dangers in the home.
Poems entitled 'Fire and flame'.
A description: 'Our visit to the fire station'.
A large frieze on 'The Great Fire of London'.
Large paintings of candle flames to illustrate the theme.
Candles: how do they burn?
Finding out how different fabrics burn.

His materials consist of:

A box of six candles.
A collection of offcuts of fabrics from the school sewing box.
Many large and small jars and bottles.
Adequate supplies of paper.
Tempera paints.
Brushes.

The plan opposite shows how he intends to organize the classroom.

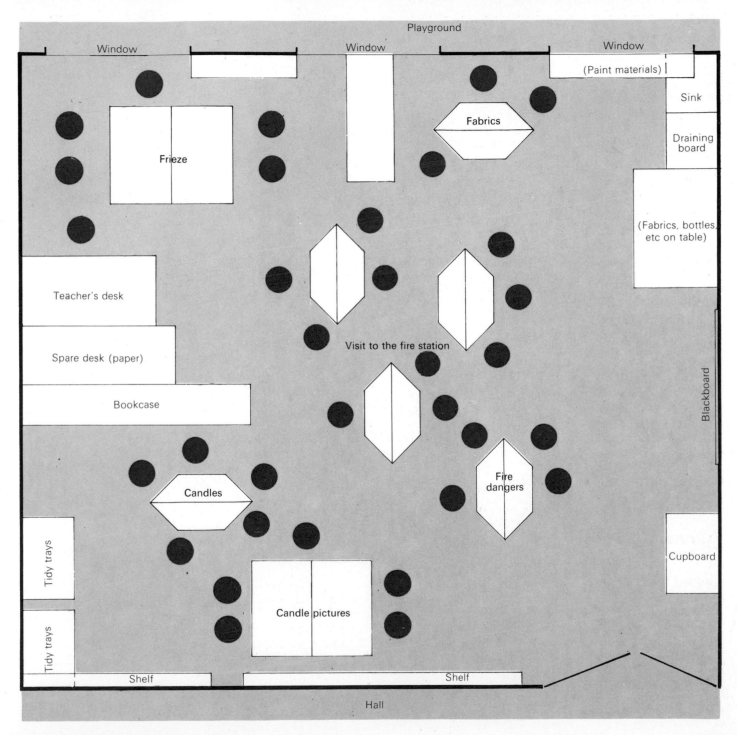

Playground

Window · Window · Window

(Paint materials)

Sink

Draining board

Frieze

Fabrics

(Fabrics, bottles, etc on table)

Teacher's desk

Spare desk (paper)

Bookcase

Visit to the fire station

Fire dangers

Candles

Tidy trays

Tidy trays

Candle pictures

Cupboard

Blackboard

Shelf · Shelf

Hall

7

Given a classroom of a similar type and children of the same age, consider in less detail:

Teacher *B,* who has a time-tabled science session every Thursday afternoon. He prefers to divide the children into small groups, each doing quite distinct activities which are not related by a theme.

This week he has decided that two groups will 'do' candle flames and air.

Teacher *C,* who has a similar time-tabled science session, is going to divide the whole class into groups, all of whom will be doing the same candle activities.

Teacher *D,* who wants to start off a small group of children on candle activities in odd moments—particularly in the gaps before play when some children have finished their other assignments. If things go well he may bring further children in as and when the opportunity arises.

Bearing in mind the need to maintain adequate supervision and control, which of these (or other) methods would *you* choose for your own class situation? Which method or methods have you used? What problems or advantages have you experienced?

Making observations about lighted candles

3 Observation

Observation of a lighted candle

You will need:

Candles, candle-stands, matches, newspaper
Small mirrors, eg squares from mirror tiles (cheap and
relatively safe)
Painting materials: paper, felt pens in suitable colours,
paints, paint pots, water, water pots, brushes
Coloured pencils, etc

Careful observation is a basic tool of science. In
CHEM study, an American science project, fifty-three
distinct observations of the candle or its flame were
listed (see bibliography: 17). Here is a challenge. With
the candle alight in front of you, see how many
observations you can make. As you make them, keep a
record. On the basis of your observations consider
these points.

Observation and the senses   We live in a
culture which places great emphasis on seeing, but of
course we make use of other senses in observation.

What observations did you make that used senses other
than sight? If you made very few observations of this
kind it is worth returning to the candle to try to add to
your list. For example, can you make use of the senses
of smell and touch? Can the candle flame produce a
sound?

Observation and interpretation   Observation
may not simply be a question of noting what the senses
tell you; there may be some interpretation involved.

Consider the following statements:

'There is something running down the side of the candle.'
'A colourless liquid is running down the side of the candle.'
'Melted wax is running down the side of the candle.'

Which of these, if any, is 'pure' observation, and which
involves some interpretation on your part? Do any of
these statements go so far beyond the evidence of the
senses that they don't really qualify as observations?

Look through your own list and check to see if your
observations are all supported by information from the
use of the senses.

See bibliography: 13.

Observation and checking   Accurate observation
depends upon the observer continually trying to match
the information he receives through his senses with his
own statements. It is an active process which may often
involve checking one observation against another, or one
made from a different viewpoint.

For example, the flame may appear from one position
not to touch the wick at all. It is possible to check this
by looking at the flame from different directions. This
is a kind of experiment, but is better distinguished from
experiment proper which involves some deliberate
control of the conditions. Consider your own
observations; to what extent did they involve 'checking'?

Why science? Observation and art   Some of
the value of doing science comes from the use of its
methods in other fields, and observation can make a
contribution to work in art.

In her book *Art in the Primary School* (see bibliography: 18) Kay Melzi says: 'Children who have acquired the habit of really searching observation will learn to see the visual world with greater understanding.'

Her approach is to provide interesting, attractive objects for the children to draw or paint. She points out, however, that this does not mean 'a return to formal object drawing with its emphasis on skills of accurate representation: the aim is more to develop powers of perception and originality.'

In its turn, of course, the desire to produce an attractive, satisfying effect may help to stimulate one's powers of observation.

Observing and painting the candle flame

Do some candle pictures yourself with oils, water colours, or felt-tip pens. You might do as accurate and as photographic a picture of the flame and the top part of the candle as possible, with it alight in front of you. The following questions may help as you observe the candle:

Is the flame bright all over? Where do you see it brightest?

What colours can you see, and where are they?

Hold up a piece of newsprint and try to look at it through the flame. Can you read it? If so, where?

What shape is the flame? Does it come to a point at the top?

What happens when you blow gently at the flame?

What shape is the wick? What does it look like?

How would you describe the appearance at the top of the candle when it is alight?

To what extent, if at all, did painting contribute to your observation? To what extent did the questions above help your observation?

See bibliography: 17, 18.

Picture-making by children

Of course, there are limits to the extent to which picture-making can be of help in stimulating observation. This may often depend upon the age and stage of development of the children. Three stages which Kay Melzi describes in the development of children's ability to make pictures are:

Scribbling This is more an exercise for the child to gain facility with the pencil or brush. Very little resemblance is discernible between the object and the picture.

Symbolism The picture is used more as a symbol of the child's idea of the object than to show what it is really like.

Visual realism There is now a closer and more detailed resemblance between the object and the picture of it.

Peter (4)

Matthew J-6

(Anthony Johnston age 9)

At what stage or stages are the children who drew these pictures? At what stage, then, do you think picture-making is likely to help in observation?

Make use of the candle and its flame (or any of the activities suggested in this book) to develop children's powers of observation by discussion and questioning.

How acute is children's observation? Do you find your questions a help or a hindrance? Where appropriate, introduce painting—possibly extending this to other objects, for example, snails, insects, flowers, shells. Does the painting help? If so, how?

See bibliography: 18.

4 Explanation

People seldom think how imaginative a process science can be. As Faraday himself put it:

'I hope you will always remember that whenever a result happens, especially if it be new, you should say: What is the cause? Why does this occur?'

As he suggests, observation raises questions, and these invite the use of imagination to provide satisfying explanations.

Experiments with candle wax

You will need:

Candle wax (from candles)
Safe method of providing cold, warm and hot water
Laboratory thermometers (short form, 0°C to 100°C+)
Heat-resistant water-containers, eg odd cups
Dusters
Candles, stands, matches
Smooth tin-lids, etc
Glass tubing (3-5 mm internal diameter, say 10-15 cm lengths, rounded edges)
Bottle, dish, or glass microscope slide for holding in flame
Newspaper

Try out the following activities. As you do so try to explain your observations; you may also find the questions helpful.

1   Manipulate some bits of wax in your hand. Notice exactly what happens. What factors caused the change, if any?

Can you get it really soft? Can you make it *melt*?

2   Drop small bits of cold candle wax into cold, warm and hot water. *With care* use a laboratory thermometer to find the temperatures. How could you find the melting point of wax?

Note: wait until the column of liquid stops moving before you read the temperature. There is no need to shake the thermometer.

3   Run a little candle wax from a burning candle:

Into hot water.
Into cold water.
To spread out on warm and cold surfaces, for example, saucers or tin-lids.

What factors decide whether the wax is liquid or solid? Are the effects of warming and cooling candle wax like, or unlike, the changes of ice to water and vice versa?

4 Blow the flame out and watch at once. What do you see?

How is what you observe like steam coming from a kettle? In what ways are they unlike? What makes the special smell of a candle when it is just blown out?

5 Light, blow out, and then relight the candle quickly, putting a flame closer and closer to the wick. What happens?

Is there any comparison here with lighting the gas from a gas ring?

Does the same thing happen if you do this to a candle that has not been alight for some time?

6 Hold a cold glass surface (bottle, dish, microscope slide) just above the wick in a candle flame for a few seconds. What do you see on the glass when you take it out?

What do you see when you blow out the candle?

7 Can you lead anything out of the flame, using a piece of glass tubing as in the diagram below? Can you light anything at the top end? Did you see anything in the tube?

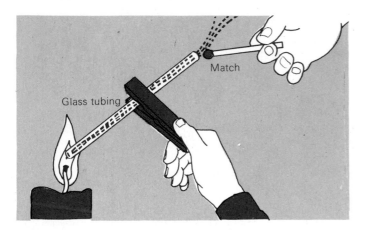

Consider the two following ideas:

Evaporation as the change of a liquid (like water) into a gas (like water vapour).
Condensation as the change of a gas back into a liquid.

Try to make use of these to help explain your observations in nos. 4–7 above.

Ideas or explanations?

It is important here to distinguish between ideas and explanations. Explanations are interpretations of *specific events*. These explanations, however, make use of ideas which can be applied in all sorts of other situations. Thus the formation of wax on a glass slide which has been placed in a candle flame is explained as the condensation of wax vapour or gas on a cold surface. *Condensation* is an example of one general idea that is of use in this explanation.

To what extent do the ideas of condensation and evaporation help you in *your* explanations of the specific observations of changes in candle wax?

Types of explanation

Those who, as pupils, have passed through a school science course might often be excused for thinking that an idea or an explanation takes only one, highly abstract, form. In fact they can take many different forms and levels of complexity. The following are some examples based on changes in candle wax. There are many other possibilities.

1 Describing 'like situations'
Teacher: 'What did you see when you blew out the candle?'
Catherine (aged eight): 'The smoke was a grey colour. It comes from the red bit. *Like when the smoke comes off the tea.*'

Catherine's explanation uses a comparison with *another concrete situation*. Refer back to your experiments on candle wax, particularly nos. 3, 5, 6 and 7. Do the comparisons suggested there help *you* to explain your observations?

Here is another example of the use of a comparison. Mark (aged eight) describes a flame: 'When you stop blowing, the air is not strong enough to hold it and it comes back. It's like a spring.'

2   Linking different factors together

Teacher: 'What happened when the candle blew out?'
Nicholas (aged ten): 'It went over to one side and smoked black smoke from the flame, grey from the wick.'
Teacher: 'Why is it *grey*?'
Nicholas: *Because it's cooler. The wick is wet when you blow it out. It's damp.'*

Nicholas here seems to be linking together certain factors (coolness, wetness and greyness) as if he sees that there is some significant relationship.

He may be quite happy with this explanation, but he may not. How might you go on from here? Catherine's comments may give you an idea.

Notice how full and accurate Nicholas's observations were. Refer back to your experiments nos. 1 and 3 on candle wax where you were asked to identify the factors involved in the changes you observed.

3   Using generalizations

Student (just after blowing out the candle): 'What's happening here?'
Peter: 'Paraffin wax is dissolving into the air.'
Student: 'Dissolving?'
Peter: 'Not dissolving, er—evaporating.'
Other juniors: 'Melting from the heat. It's watery.'
Peter: 'A liquid, then it evaporates.'
Others: 'A white gas, smoke fumes.'

Notice, in this example, the discussion about the relative merits of the generalizations 'evaporating' and 'dissolving'. Perhaps Peter had seen a possible similarity between what was happening to the wax vapour and the way in which sugar or other substances can be 'seen' to dissolve in water.

How did the discussion *among* the children help here?

How did the student influence the direction which the discussion took?

Here are some generalizations which can help to explain the observations on pages 12-14:

Solids when heated melt to give liquids, for example, butter, ice, candle wax.
Liquids when cooled 'set' to give solids, for example, water → ice.
Liquids when heated evaporate to give gases, for example, water → water vapour.
Gases when cooled condense to give liquids, for example, steam → water.

4   Trying to explain 'how'

The above do *nothing* to explain the link between the amount of heat put in and the condition of the substance. To take this further it becomes necessary to use explanations which go beyond what can be observed, for example:

Solids like ice or wax consist of minute particles called molecules packed closely together and attracting each other. A solid therefore retains its shape.

Heating such a solid causes the molecules to move about faster and to separate. The separated molecules are not so strongly attached to one another and have no fixed position. The solid has melted to produce a liquid. Cooling reverses this process and causes the liquid to turn back into a solid.

Continued heating of a liquid causes the molecules to move even faster, to the extent of shooting off and *evaporating* into the surrounding air to produce a gas, for example, steam from a kettle, or wax vapour from a hot wick. In a gas the molecules are very widely separated and free to move in all directions.

The effect of cooling a gas is to slow the molecules down so that they come together, the substance *condensing* into a liquid again.

See bibliography: 16.

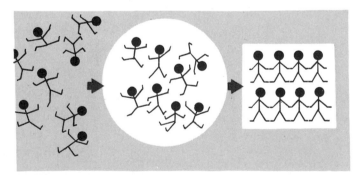

A child was interested in the way in which water 'disappeared' from a flat saucer that had been left on the shelf. He was only eight. Which method of explanation would you and he be most likely to use in the ensuing discussion? What specific form might these explanations take? Method 4 involves rather abstract ideas, but would you completely discount its use?

Misconceptions

What attitude should we have to children's misconceptions? Consider:

Elizabeth, who did this drawing of a candle which had just been blown out to show where the 'water' comes from. She had observed the colourless liquid in the top of the candle, and had seen how it dripped when the lighted candle was tilted. Her circles are drops of 'water'. The tiny circle by the wick is the hole which lets the 'water' out when the candle was held sloping downwards. This, anyway, is Elizabeth's explanation.

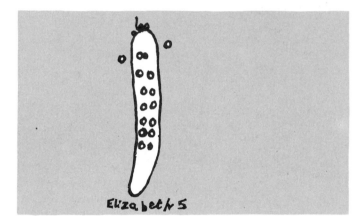

Perry (aged six) seems to be saying something similar.

Teacher: 'What's the stuff dripping off the candle?'
Perry: 'Water.'
Teacher: 'Where does it come from?'
Perry: 'It comes out of the black thing—at the bottom. It squeezes out when it's lighted.'
Teacher: 'Where is the water?'
Perry: 'It's inside the black thing.'
Teacher: 'Is it really water?'
Perry: 'Yes.'
Teacher: 'Can you drink it?'
Perry: 'No.'
Teacher: 'Why?'
Perry: 'Because it's too burny . . .'
Teacher: 'What will happen to the water?'
Perry: 'It'll dry up.'

What do you think Elizabeth and Perry mean when they use the word 'water'? Do they understand the idea that solid wax can change into a liquid?

Does Elizabeth perhaps see some relationship between the candle and a 'squeezy' bottle full of liquid?' If so, she seems to be fitting her explanation to this idea disconcertingly well; for example, there *is* a hole at the base of the wick.

Thinks . . .

Another conversation, with Nicholas (aged ten), shows a different type of misconception.

Teacher: 'Do you mean it [the wax] dries like water?'
Nicholas: 'No, it dries hard quicker and if you put your finger in the wax it dries ever so quickly.'
Teacher: 'Yes, why would it dry quicker if you put your finger in it?'
Nicholas: 'Because your finger's warm.'
Teacher: 'So presumably if it was on a cold surface it wouldn't dry so quickly?'
Nicholas: 'No.'

What other factor, that might also affect the speed at which wax hardens, has Nicholas left out here?

There are a number of ways of tackling these misconceptions. The teacher may:

Ask questions, and/or suggest some simple practical tests, to help the children reconsider their explanations. What questions/tests can you think of that might help?

Give the children a direct explanation.
Accept the children's explanations.

The choice may be influenced by the following points:

Stage of development   The children may be quite unready to modify their ideas. On the other hand questioning *may* show that they are aware of inadequacies in these explanations.

The 'right' explanation?   An explanation is effective only in so far as it fits observations into a pattern which has some meaning for the person concerned. What is 'right' for the teacher may not necessarily be 'right' for the child. In any case, is any explanation ever completely 'right'?

What choice or choices would you make with Elizabeth, Perry and Nicholas?

It is important that children should be given the chance *and the freedom* to work out their own explanations. It is only in this way that the teacher is able to start where *they are*—rather than where he thinks they ought to be.

It is useful to keep a record—if only a mental one—of interesting explanations and ideas.

For example, what different types of explanation do you find children using? To what extent do they make use of like situations to explain their observations?

Do you find that some, despite their limited experience, are extremely imaginative, to the extent in fact where you say 'I would never have thought of that myself!'

5 Experiment: a case history

In science it is important that we should try to find out if our explanations fit the facts. Sometimes this can be done by straightforward observation. Often, however, it may be necessary to control the conditions artificially by means of an experiment. The following discussion gives a good idea of the general features of the experimental process. But it also shows something of the highly individual and imaginative thought that goes into working out a *particular* experiment.

Mark's good idea

Mark is eight and goes to a Kent primary school. The school is situated near a large market town and most of the children are drawn from a large new estate of semi-detached council and private houses nearby.

Mark's teacher rates him as poor at writing and average at number. She also remarked—rather affectionately—that he is 'a bit of a nuisance'. He is a good example of the kind of child, by no means rare in primary schools, whose enquiring and creative mind is apparent more from his general behaviour than his attainment in the normal classroom subjects. Such children are invaluable to the teacher introducing science into the classroom for the first time.

Transcript, first section
Mark: When the wax dries will it disintegrate or will it stay there until it's wiped off?
Teacher: 'Well, that's something you'll have to watch and see, isn't it? I say, I tell you what, wouldn't it be a good idea if you took a piece like that away with you and watched it to see what happened to it? And how could you tell . . . whether . . . ?'
Mark: 'Well, when you get home you could measure

it—measure the length—and each day you could measure the length again and again and you could see if it was getting smaller . . .'
Teacher: 'You could see if it was getting smaller.'
Mark: 'Is it stuck or is it staying the same size?'
Teacher: 'Yes—so—now how would you measure it? Let's see. What would you measure it with?'
Mark: 'A ruler.'
Teacher: 'Yes. Hang on, let's just get a ruler. Right, those are centimetres, right. Let's put it up against the ruler. That's right . . .'
Mark: 'One and three-quarters.'
Teacher: 'One and three-quarter centimetres, so you've got to wrap it up pretty carefully otherwise you'll break bits off it. So if you remember that. . . . Let's write it down.'

Consideration of first section

Mark has thought of two alternative explanations. Either the wax will 'disintegrate' or it will 'stay there'. The experiment starts with Mark and the teacher deciding on a *hypothesis*.

This is a statement, based on the explanations, which is phrased so that it can be put to practical test. Sometimes it is called an 'if . . . then . . .' statement. In this case, it would be: *'If* wax disintegrates *then* it will get smaller if I leave it for a while.'

So far Mark is interested in only one factor or variable (here, change in size) and he has not suggested any factors which might cause the disintegration.

Is Mark's method of measurement adequate?

Transcript, second section

Mark: 'I could wrap it up in that if you don't mind.' (Mark wraps the wax in a piece of paper.)
Teacher: 'There you are, so it's one and three-quarter centimetres.'
Mark: 'Thank you.'
Teacher: 'Yes. It's a very good idea, that. All right. You could keep it here, couldn't you, and measure it every day to see what happens to it? I tell you one thing, though. Would it be right to keep it wrapped up in paper . . . if you're going to try to find out if it goes away?'

Mark: 'No, I wouldn't have thought so because the air may make it disintegrate and if it doesn't get in it may stay the same size and then you won't find out.'
Teacher: 'That's right. So in fact when you take it home you'd have to put it out somewhere in the air to see what happens to it, wouldn't you?'

Consideration of second section

Mark's explanation is now modified to suggest that disintegration might be caused by the air. His hypothesis would now be: *'If* this is so *then* the wax will get smaller when I leave it open to the air.'

But is his practical test now completely 'fair'? If not, why not? Assuming that the length of the wax were found to decrease, what other factors or variables apart from the air might have caused the change?

Note the effect of a quite accidental event (wrapping the wax up) in the course of the experiment.

Transcript, third section

Mark: 'Here, I've got a good idea. When you get home if I take some wax off an old candle which we didn't finish in the power cut . . . well, I could put one wrapped up in paper and one in the air to see which happened to both of them.'
Teacher: 'That's a good idea, isn't it? What about the size of the wax that you took from the candle? If you wanted to see what the difference was would they be different sizes or the same size?'
Mark: 'Well, more or less the same size, as close as I could get.'
Teacher: 'Yes. That's a very good idea!'

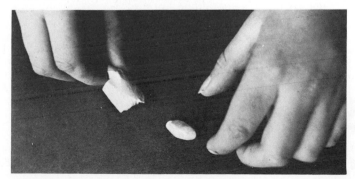

Consideration of third section 'Here, I've got a good idea!' And he had! This is a good attempt to control the conditions, in order to separate the effect of air from that of other variables that might produce the disintegration.

What other suggestions might you make to Mark to help ensure that the test really was fair?

Mark wrote this description a week later. What has he added?

'My exsperment with wax'
'I am trying to find out what will happen with two pieces of wax one has liht and that is shrinking one has no air or light that iscent doing anything each $\frac{3}{4}$ of an inch the one that isnt getting any light or air is rapped up in paper.'

What would be your response to his comment that one piece of wax *did* shrink?

See bibliography: 10.

Why science? For its own sake?

Science 5/13 points out:

'Teachers will find that the objectives we have selected are most easily and, in some cases, only achieved when children are actively investigating problems which are genuinely their own and are doing work which involves real discovery with all the excitement and meaning this has for them.'

Mark's 'experiment' is a good demonstration of the truth of this statement. On the other hand, too much stress may be placed on science being done to satisfy particular purposes, often those of the teacher.

Perhaps we also ought to appreciate—as Mark obviously did—that science is simply worth doing for its own sake: no other justification is necessarily needed.

Objectives

Below is a section from a list of science objectives from Schools Council Science 5/13. In this case, at least, which objectives have been achieved and which, possibly, are close to being realized?

Posing questions and devising experiments or investigations to answer them
Stage 1 Transition from intuition to concrete operations.
Infants generally
1.41 Ability to find answers to simple problems by investigation.
1.42 Ability to make comparisons in terms of one property or variable.

Concrete operations. Early stage.
1.43 Appreciation of the need for measurement.
1.44 Awareness that more than one variable may be involved in a particular change.

Stage 2 Concrete operations. Later stage.
2.41 Ability to frame questions likely to be answered through investigations.
2.42 Ability to investigate variables and to discover effective ones.
2.43 Appreciation of the need to control variables and use controls in investigations.
2.44 Ability to choose and use either arbitrary or standard units of measurement as appropriate.
2.45 Ability to select a suitable degree of approximation and work to it.
2.46 Ability to use representational models for investigating problems or relationships.

Stage 3 Transition to stage of abstract thinking.
3.41 Attempting to identify the essential steps in approaching a problem scientifically.
3.42 Ability to design experiments with effective controls for testing hypotheses.
3.43 Ability to visualize a hypothetical situation as a useful simplification of actual observations.
3.44 Ability to construct scale models for investigation and to appreciate implications of changing the scale.

How would you rate Mark's scientific thinking? Will his ability be recognized in the future?

6 Experiment: a fair test?

The 'candle in the jar' experiment

You will need:

Matches, candles (three per experiment).
Three colourless glass jars, similar in shape (say coffee jars) but as different in size as possible. The smallest must still be tall enough to go over a candle without the flame touching the glass.
Stands, water, water-measuring apparatus (graduated jar or jug?).
Clock with sweep second hand, or stop clock.
Dish (eg large soup plate or plastic sandwich box).
For students: Ladybird Junior Science book *Air, Wind and Flight* (see bibliography: 2).

It would be absurd to expect children always to work out ideas for experiments by themselves. To do so would be to expect them to discover fresh knowledge which has been gathered together over many years. The teacher will also have to make use of ideas from himself or herself, other people and books. Sometimes these provide a start from which the more spontaneous questions like those of Mark will arise.

But when experiments come from books there are certain dangers. First, the teacher will have to be careful not to let his or her knowledge of the likely outcome stifle unexpected observations or explanations by children. Secondly, 'textbook' explanations of standard experiments are often imperfect or incomplete, even if printed.

1 Take an old experiment, step by step
a. Burn two equal candles side by side; stand an inverted colourless (say coffee) jar over one. (Don't use any water yet—it isn't necessary and only complicates things.)

Watch carefully; you will see several things happen, but one will be more significant than the others.

Explain the results to yourself. The common explanation is that 'The candle in the jar goes out because it's used up all the air/oxygen.'

See what Peter (aged ten) thinks:

Student: 'How would you put a candle flame out?'
Juniors: 'Snuff it—blow it.'
Peter: 'Use a snuffer: It just snuffs it because there's no air getting into it. See, it burns up oxygen and without oxygen it can't burn, because it suffocates like people. It needs air to burn, like a person needs air to breathe.'

To test this explanation further:

b. Light the same two candles and try two jars of very different sizes simultaneously. Are the results what you expected? Could the effects be timed? Would once be enough? What precautions would be needed between experiments to give the candle flame 'fresh' air?

c. Now with three candles and a seconds timer, try large, medium and small jars, all at once. Is there a relationship between time of burning and size of jar? How could the volume of air in each jar be found? Could a graph be usefully drawn?

Consider this activity as an example of a controlled experiment. It starts with a 'folk-belief'—from books or children—but it is not accepted without checking.

An experiment is carried out treating two candle flames differently, and we *observe results*. If the explanation is like Peter's, our *hypothesis* might be that: '*If* without oxygen a candle can't burn, *then* the candle will go out.' (See *a*.)

We think we can explain these results, so the explanation is tested in a slightly different experiment. What is the hypothesis on which this experiment is based? (See *b*.)

This either agrees with what we expected, or does not; in either case we *test again*.

This time we add *measuring* to the experiment; the results of measuring can often be understood, and communicated to others, better by a graph than by written figures. (See *c*.)

2 Next try the usual 'textbook' version

Stand a lighted candle in a dish, pour in some water and cover the candle with a jar or milk bottle, watching carefully right from the beginning.

The hypothesis here usually goes: '*If* burning uses up all the oxygen, and if water displaces any gas used, *then* the water will rise to occupy the space left unoccupied.'

Mark (aged eight) said 'It's causing bubbles!' Do you find this?

3 Try to explain further   Repeat 1*a*. and feel:

The heat round the flame in the open.
The top of the jar as its candle goes out.

What things happen to air when it is heated? Would an effect of heat on air account for Mark's observation above? If so, how and why? What extra factor must one now take into account?

How far does the effect of heat that Mark noticed change the simple explanation quoted in 1*a*.? Need the candle have used up any oxygen at all to produce a rise of water in the jar? (Look back at the evidence.)

4   Study very carefully pages 12 and 13 of the Ladybird Junior Science book *Air, Wind and Flight*. Make your own assessment of the text page 'Air and burning' and the illustration opposite it. Look for descriptions of the same experiment in other books.

Note: Dr Kempa says (with experimental evidence) in *Science Teaching Techniques No. 12* that candle flames do *not* use up all the oxygen, but only one-third of it. This leaves 14 per cent oxygen in the jar; a candle will not burn with less oxygen than this, he says.

See bibliography: 2, 11, 13.

Why teach science?

This is an example of an experiment which at first glance seems clear-cut, but it is by no means so simple and unambiguous. Experiments are often said to 'prove' a hypothesis; in fact there is considerable doubt if this is possible. But it is a different matter to say, 'The results of this experiment support my hypothesis. I will accept it cautiously until I obtain evidence to the contrary.'

Consider, for example, the arguments for and against fluoridation of drinking water, in which protagonists claim scientific 'proof' on both sides.

See bibliography: 25.

7 Where has all the candle gone?

Explanations of how a candle burns

The usual explanation of how a candle burns is:

1   The heat from the flame of the match melts the wax, already on the wick; this wax then evaporates.

2   The temperature of the flame ignites the wax vapour, which begins to burn.

3   The heat from the burning wax melts more wax at the base of the wick.

4   This liquid wax travels up the wick by capillary action (like water up a string) where it evaporates and burns.

Children, like most adults, find this difficult to grasp, mainly because little of this can actually be observed.

Some difficulties are that:

1   Some wax oftens runs down the side and remains unburnt as the candle is used, and it is assumed that this represents *all* of the original wax.

2   Normally wax does not burn if a flame is applied to it as Nicholas (aged ten) suggests in this connection:

Teacher: 'Will wax burn by itself?'
Nicholas: 'No, it wouldn't burn—it would just melt.'

This leads to the question 'Then what is wax for?' to which children give some very sensible replies.

Mark (aged eight): 'To keep the wick inside, otherwise if you didn't have wax the wick would just drop over.'
Suzanne (aged seven): 'So it doesn't burn.'
Teacher: 'So that what doesn't burn?'
Suzanne: 'The wax.'
Lucy (aged seven): 'To stop the house catching alight.'
Claire (aged eight): 'Because the string [wick] will just burn and burn and burn and it won't take very long to burn out.'

3   The wick so obviously does burn that no other explanation is felt to be necessary. However, there is much surprise when a black piece of burnt match (which appears not to burn at all) gives an excellent flame when used as a substitute wick.

Mark: 'Suppose it's . . . is there anything inside wax, or is wax just wax?'
Nicholas (an equally thoughtful explanation): 'Perhaps it's the wax. Perhaps they both go together and they make . . .'

4   The movement of liquid wax up the wick is, to say the least, not obvious.

It therefore seems that most children and many adults may assume that wax plays no direct role in burning. On the other hand the children often come across observations which give a clue to the nature of this process: these often emerge from activities like those in the following chapter.

The role of the teacher might therefore be to prompt discussion and possibly further activity, not so much to teach children *about the process* as to develop observation, imaginative explanation and experiment.

Candles as clocks

You will need:

Thin and thick candles, candle-stands, matches, tapers.
Plasticine, newspaper.
Clock with sweep second hand if possible, or stop clock.
Pins, rulers (method of marking candle wax).
As much as desired of apparatus shown for candle clocks in Schools Council Science 5/13 *Time*, pages 19-20 (see bibliography: 9).

Pupils may already have met the idea of the candle clock—but possibly not in practice—during work in mathematics (King Alfred, etc). Some other types of clock are suggested in *Time*, pages 16–21, 43. Start the children with only one kind of candle to establish the time/length burnt relationship.

1 Using a single candle, consider practically the following problems:

Method of measurement How will you measure the candle? Will you measure the total length before and after a time lapse, or by marking a candle in equal units? Should these units be arbitrary (any convenient length) or standard (for example in centimetres)?

Setting the candle up If a unit method is decided upon, how will the divisions be marked? Try using scratches, spirit-based felt tip, or lipstick, and pins stuck in lightly at equal intervals.

Marking candles

2 Compare the rates of burning down of a taper (upright in a Plasticine base), a thin candle and a thick candle. What is the main variable here: the thickness (diameter) of the candle—or what?

Children's predictions of which will burn down the fastest, and their explanations of why, may vary, Of the shortest (but also the fattest) candle in the group, a child may say:

'It's short—so it'll burn the quickest.' Here the important variable is considered to be the height.

'It may burn slower because . . . there's more of it.' Here emphasis is placed on the *quantity* of wax.

Mark (aged eight): 'If the wax is the same it'll probably burn at the same rate, if there's the same amount. If there's not the same amount, the one that's got the less will probably burn the fastest.'

What does Mark mean here by 'amount'? Which type of explanation or explanations is he closest to?

3 Consider practically what other variables might influence the rate at which a candle burns down. Children have a habit of noticing the less obvious ones.

Teacher: 'Of a candle and a nightlight, which will burn down the faster?'
Mark, again: 'The tall candle.'
Teacher: 'Why?'
Mark: 'It's got a larger wick!'

You and they will also come across situations which will interfere with the normal teacher/child assumption that a candle clock is likely to burn away the same length of candle/taper per unit time.

Children may well find several ways of making candle clocks go faster (draughts, 'drains', etc) and one or two ways of making them go slower (for example, flooding).

Organization: the time interval

One special problem is the length of time it takes before any result is achieved. The questions, therefore, are:

What will you and the children do in the intervening time? Where will the burning candle be placed?

For quick results use half tapers, held upright in small mounds of Plasticine.

What methods of measurement, and possibly of marking the candle, do you find the most effective?

What predictions do the children make when comparing the rates of burning of candles of different sizes?

How do you cope with the problem of the long time interval?

Did any unexpected variables make the candle clocks go wrong? If so, which ones?

Where has all the candle gone?

You will need:

Short candle, matches, ruler
Old saucer
Slide projector (or sunshine!)
White paper/wall
Small simple balance (eg letter scales) or weighing apparatus as in Schools Council Science 5/13 *Time*, page 20

1 Candle clocks usually estimate passage of time by measuring *length* of candle burnt; try the *weight* alternative shown in *Time*, page 20, or invent one.

Classroom scales or balances are probably quite accurate and sensitive enough to give good results. It may not be safe to weigh the candle while it is burning.

Would a weighed candle give as good a result as a 'measured' one? Should one catch and include any wax which runs down the side? Ask children.

2 If you have the opportunity, test the accuracy of a 'length' method compared with a 'weight' method of using a candle as a clock. Think out ways in which each of these may be inaccurate and ways in which each could be made *more accurate*.

3 What gets away in the candle's loss of weight? For a clue to what happens, try cooling the top half of the flame with a cold saucer. What comes out of the flame? Could it have come from anywhere but the wax?

If the flame is not cooled, the wax burns away totally.

4 To watch the final products getting away, put a lighted candle in sunshine or the bright beam from a projector and look at the *shadow of the flame* on a wall or vertical sheet of paper. This shadow shows two movements of gases, (a) from the flame, (b) in the air round the flame. Is the movement from the flame itself (the loss in weight) due to candle-wax vapour rising (like steam from a saucepan) or to new gases made in the flame?

The scientific activities on this page are concerned with invisible materials. How can one help children to comprehend the reality of such things as air, gas, water vapour, etc?

Ask many incidental questions about invisible materials, for example: what's in an empty bottle?

What ideas do the children seem to have? Do *they* suggest any ways of finding out?

8 Energy from candle flames

Different forms of energy

You will need:

Matches and matchboxes (different kinds)
Candles and stands
Damp newspaper
Medium wire, corks on bits of raw potato, etc (as 'handles')
Frying or olive oil, suet, cooking fat
Aluminium foil cases from mince-pies or small fancy cakes
Thick cotton string, scissors
Nightlights

1 Strike a match; you put some *energy* into striking it on a rough surface. Why does it need a rough surface? What *starts* the match-head burning?
(It can't be the chemicals by themselves, obviously.)

See bibliography: 12.

2 Light the candle; this involves giving some energy to the wick. Observe carefully.

What *three things* does the *heat energy* supplied by the burning match do to the wax in the wick?

3 The candle flame gives out some energy of its own. The flame can be *seen*, and *felt*. Three kinds of energy come from a flame. Can you name them?

4 Hold your hand *beside* the flame and feel the heat; then try it *above* the flame—starting high. This gives the clue to the third kind of energy set free: something moves, upwards rather than sideways.

5 Try burning a little frying oil or suet or cooking fat in an aluminium mince-pie case with a thick cotton-string wick.

Compare this 'lamp' with a nightlight, for size of flame, amount of light and safety.

6 To test the heat in a candle flame, use fairly thick wire, holding it across at different levels. How long would you hold it there? Why is it important to hold it at *different* levels?

Maybe a cork as a 'handle' would help. Why?

(Student asks the children what happens to the wire.) Juniors: 'It's going brown, and it gets brighter and brighter and brighter.'

Do you find the same results as they did? Do you see more? How do you explain them to yourself?

How far can, and should, such science activities in class be used to help children to deal with their environment (home, camp, etc) more safely? How do you see the relative importance of fixed rules and guided experience (as above)?

What have you found that struck you about (a) children's ideas of safety, and (b) the risks children face?

Devise ways of helping them to see and avoid danger sensibly.

The brightness of candle light

You will need:

Several kinds of paper (brown, greaseproof, etc)
Five candles, candle-stands, matches, newspaper
Electric torch, ruler(s)
Method of holding paper vertical (stand and clips)
Graph paper
Partial blackout if possible

1 With a little *hot* melted wax, make a round grease-spot on a piece of paper, so that the spot looks definitely darker than the rest when it is on the table/bench. Hold it up to the light. How would you describe the spot now? (What effect has the wax really had on the transparency of the paper?) How was this used in the Middle Ages?

Now use this as 'Bunsen's grease-spot photometer'. (This is the same Professor Bunsen who invented the laboratory gas-burner. He was the first professor who had all his students doing practical work in the

Working with the grease-spot photometer

laboratory, too ; before his time they only watched demonstration experiments.)

2 Light *two* candles and hold the grease-spot vertically between the flames, moving it to and fro until you can hardly see the spot.

How does the spot look against a *dark* background ? And how does it look with the light behind it ? Now it looks almost invisible ; what does this say about the light from the two candle flames ?

(Student pours drops of wax onto paper.)
Juniors : 'It looks black on that paper, like all holes in it because the wax melted through . . . it's soaked through.'
(Student holds up paper.)
Juniors : 'It's gone transparent. You can't see exactly through it. The fat's like oil . . . does it dry up when it's finished ? You get the light from one side, and it glows . . . [with two candles on one side] it glows more.'

3 For this you need at least *three* candles—perhaps a group could do it together. Light three, and arrange them so that their flames are all at about the same level. Put one on one side of the paper with the grease-spot (still vertical, of course) and the other *two* candles close together on the other side of the photometer.

Arrange them so that the grease-spot almost disappears again ; measure the distance between the single candle and the paper, and between the paper and the two candles.

What did you think you would find ? Did you find it ? Can you try again with *four* candles together on one side, with one on the other side ? Measure again. Get others to try this experiment too. It is quite difficult to decide where the exact position of the grease-spot should be.

In activities 2 and 3 the aim is to change only *one variable*. What precautions might be needed ?

4 The two measurements—number of candles, and distance from grease-spot—are exactly, but not simply, connected. Can you find a relationship between them ?

See bibliography : 1.

Using candle light

You will need :

Candle and stand, magnifying glass (as large as possible), white paper (*not* ceiling tile) screen, and method of holding it vertical
If available, round-bottomed flask, water and stand
Tin (say 16–20 oz bean or fruit tin), nail (say 3 in), hammer
Greaseproof or tracing paper, rubber bands, newspaper
Two mirrors, aluminium kitchen foil, scissors
Any available reflectors from torches, head lamps, etc
Partial blackout if possible

1 People have been using candle-type lamps, burning oil or fat with a wick, for thousands of years. What are the advantages of candles for lighting ? And what are the disadvantages ? (The Science Museum's booklet *Lighting 1* has excellent historical illustrations. See bibliography : 7, and page 32.)

2 To get the light where you want it, and away from the hot flame, use a magnifying glass or a round flask of water. (*Junior Science Source Book* shows how lacemakers used just this method. See bibliography : 1.)

Above: Animal lamps and torches
Below: Lanterns

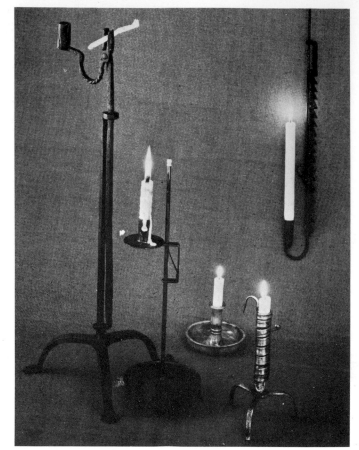

Above: Tallow candles
Below: Early candle holders

(several thicknesses) round the paper end, to keep it shaded. Point the little hole (the so-called pinhole) towards the candle flame and look into the newspaper tube at the greaseproof paper 'screen'; move the tin until you can see something clearly.

Explain to yourself what you see. Put the ideas in points nos. 2 and 3 together and compare with (a) the human eye, and (b) a simple camera. (If you can find an old box Brownie, so much the better.)

4 Put a mirror behind a candle flame. Does it make *more* light? Can you direct the light where you want it?

Test various positions of (a) one mirror, (b) two mirrors. Try a small sheet of kitchen foil curved round behind the flame. How can this foil 'copy' the effect of the reflector behind a torch bulb or car headlamp?

How far should one base science teaching on everyday life? Is there a place for teaching science which has no apparent relevance to normal experience?

What information, ideas and inventions do *children* provide for *you*? See bibliography: 4.

3 Make a 'pinhole camera' by knocking a hole in the middle of the bottom of a tin with a thin nail and fixing a piece of greaseproof paper over the open end of the tin with a rubber band. Make a tube of newspaper

9 Further possibilities based on this topic

It can sometimes be of help if you can base your planning on a pre-existing scheme of possibilities. These may consist of:

Ideas Ideas which are especially likely to be extended and clarified through study of the topic (for example, melting, capillary action).

Activities What children can *do* or try to *find out* (for example, measuring, observing).

Things Objects or phenomena that the children might usefully investigate (for example, candles, wax, flames).

A chart of possibilities

The following chart may help to give you some ideas. It can be used in conjunction with the bibliography on page 37. Each of the three sub-sections can be used quite simply as it stands. Of these, sub-section 2 is particularly useful.

Indeed, a teacher who becomes familar with the items in it can use them to stimulate discussion and investigations in any situation irrespective of the topic. For example, the use of comparison—saying to children 'What's it like?', 'What's it different from?'—is extremely productive.

1 Ideas which may emerge

Burning ⎫
Evaporation ⎪
Condensation ⎬ eg of wax
Melting ⎪
Hardening ⎭

Repulsion
  (eg of water by wax)
Safety
Solubility
Floating

Expansion/contraction
Conduction (of heat)
Convection
  (in gases/liquids)
Capillary rise
  (in wick, string, etc)

Friction/lubrication
  (eg of surfaces by wax)
Translucence
Brightness
Amount
Time

2 Activities: things children can do or try to find out

Observing
  effects of . . .
  conditions affecting . . .
  products of . . .
Considering
  uses of . . .
  history of . . .

Comparing
Measuring
Making
Drawing, modelling,
  painting, etc
Writing about
Explaining
Experimenting

3 Things: objects or phenomena which the children might investigate

Heat
Light
Colours
Air
Water
Candles and nightlights
Hallowe'en lanterns
Oil lamps
Fire and flames
Waxes and paraffins
Fuels
Wick, string, paper
Textiles
Waxed paper,
  waterproofing
Carbon, lamp black,
  potato prints
Inks, linoblocks

Wax crayons, wax soluble
  pigments
Rubbings, wax resist
  painting, batik
Lubricants and polishes
Clocks
Pinhole cameras
Flask and other lenses
Photometers
Pictures (eg postcards
  illustrating candles)
Mobiles, convection
  spirals
Quotations (eg 'Colours
  seen by candlelight will
  not look the same by
  day', Robert Browning)

Putting ideas together

Many useful ideas can come, either by putting ideas in each sub-section, or in separate sub-sections, together. In this, and other ways, a web of possibilities can be built up around a topic of interest and, if you wish, can be written down as a flow diagram. However, a flow diagram is often neither essential nor possible. Nor need it take any special form; a quickly scribbled sketch can be just as useful as the more complex construction shown below based on burning.

Using the chart of possibilities, practise making a flow diagram for yourself, based on wax, candlelight, or any other item that interests you (see page 36).

Consider the uses of some or all of these methods in practice in school.

1 Prepare plans that make use of some of the items suggested in the chart. Was the chart of any use?

2 Use your list of possibilities in a search of books and other resources. To what extent, if at all, did this make your search more profitable?

3 Use your list or flow diagram of possibilities as a basis for class or group discussion to help obtain the children's suggestions. Did this help at all? To what extent did the discussion modify your plans?

Have you any examples of good ideas that came from the children? (See bibliography: 4.)

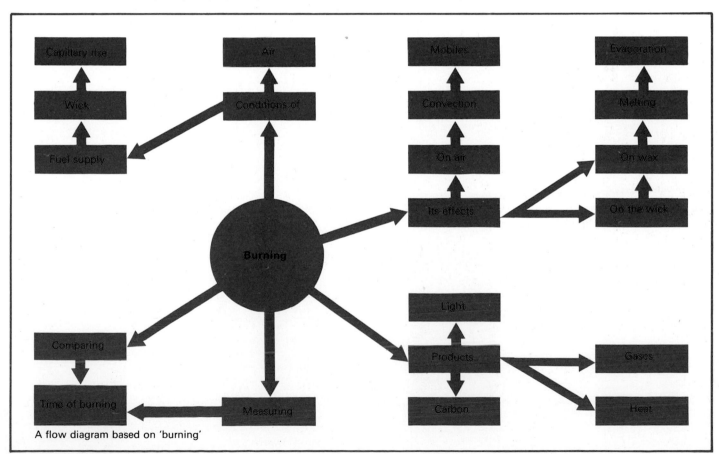

A flow diagram based on 'burning'

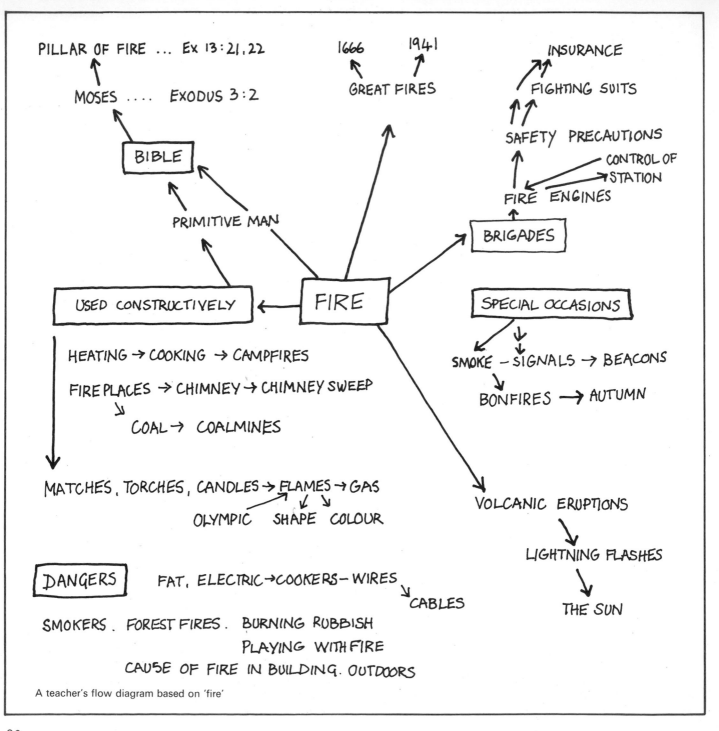

A teacher's flow diagram based on 'fire'

Bibliography

For direct work with children

1 Bainbridge, J. W., Stockdale, R. W., and Wastnedge, E. R. (1970) *Junior Science Source Book*. Collins. See pages 12, 15–21, 164, 167–169, 178, 179, 196.
2 Newing, F. E. and Bowood, Richard (1963) *Air, Wind and Flight*. Ladybird Junior Science Series. Wills and Hepworth. See pages 12–13.
3 Newing, F. E. and Bowood, Richard (1962) *Light, Mirrors and Lenses*. Ladybird Junior Science Series. Wills and Hepworth. See pages 6 and 18.
4 Nuffield Junior Science (1967) *Apparatus*. Collins. See pages 135, 142, 151, 156–157, 199–201, 220–223, 228–229.
5 Nuffield Junior Science (1967) *Teacher's Guide 1*. Collins. See pages 17–19, 27–28, 56–58, 171–174.
6 Nuffield Junior Science (1967) *Teacher's Guide 2*. Collins. See pages 167–172.
7 O'Dea, W. T. (1972) *Lighting 1: Early Oil Lamps, Candles*. (a Science Museum booklet) H.M.S.O.
8 Schools Council Science 5/13 (1972) *Change*. Macdonald Educational. See page 52.
9 Schools Council Science 5/13 (1972) *Time*. Macdonald Educational. See pages 5, 19–21, 43.
10 Schools Council Science 5/13 (1972) *With objectives in mind*. Macdonald Educational. See pages 43–45 (testing hypotheses).

For further information and ideas

11 Association for Science Education (1967) *Science Teaching Techniques No. 12*. Association for Science Education. See pages 73–74.

12 Bainbridge, Jack (1972) *Fire and flame*. Evans Bros. See pages 13-16.
13 Bassey, Michael (1969) *Science and Society: Meaning and Importance of Scientific Method*. University of London Press. See pages 34, 35, 54–55.
14 *Encyclopaedia Britannica* : candles, etc.
15 Faraday, Michael (1962) *Chemical History of a Candle*. Collier Books, New York.
16 Kuslan, L. I. and Stone, A. H. (1968) *Teaching Children Science; An Inquiry Approach*. Wadsworth. See pages 45–50, 52–55, 85–86.
17 McClellan, A. L. (ed) (1964) CHEM Study : *Chemistry: An Experimental Science*. (Teachers' guide, Unit 1.) W. H. Freeman. (Ask at a library for this book— it is expensive but interesting.)
18 Melzi, K. (1967) *Art in the Primary School*. Blackwell. See pages 4–7, 17, 61–62.
19 Nuffield Combined Science (1970) *Teachers' Guide I*. Longman. See pages 170–175.
20 Nuffield Combined Science (1970) *Teachers' Guide II*. Longman. See pages 20–22, 131–147.
21 Nuffield O-level Chemistry (1967) Background book : *Burning*. Longman.
22 Nuffield Secondary Science (1971) *Theme 7 Using Materials*. Longman. See pages 69–122 (fuels).
23 Revised Nuffield Chemistry (1975) *Teachers' guide I*. Longman. See pages 85–87. If you do not have the revised Nuffield Chemistry books, see the following : Nuffield Chemistry (1967) *Collected Experiments*. Longman. See pages 63–65.
or Nuffield Chemistry (1967) *The Sample Scheme Stages I and II : The Basic Course*. Longman. See pages 61–65.
24 Samuel, Evelyn (1968) *Introducing Batik*. Batsford. (N.B. safety.)
25 Schools Council General Studies Project (1972) *Science and Responsibility*. Longman and Penguin Education.

Acknowledgements
The authors and publishers are indebted to the following
for their invaluable help in the preparation of this book.

The children and staff of:

Southfield Middle School, London W4
Brookfield County Primary Junior School and
Brookfield County Primary Infants School, Swallow
Road, Larkfield, Kent
Regina Coeli Primary School, Pampisford Road, Purley,
Surrey

The staff and students of Thomas Huxley College of
Education, London W3

Illustration credits
Photographs
By courtesy of the Trustees of the London Museum,
page 32, bottom left and right
Crown copyright, Science Museum, London, page 32,
top left and right
Kevin Morgan, pages 2, 33
Mike Parry, page 10

Terry Williams, all other photographs

Line drawings by GWA Design Consultants

Cover design by GWA Design Consultants

Teaching 5-13 Teachers' Units

Advisory Editor: **Frank F. Blackwell**
General Inspector for Schools, London Borough of Croydon and Director of the Primary Extension Programme of the Council for Educational Technology

Teaching 5–13 is a range of books that reflect current development in education in practical terms. It provides sources of immediate help to teachers, with the liberal use of photographs and diagrams to convey information.

The range of books in *Teaching 5–13* will be wide enough to illustrate both changes in emphasis and curriculum content as the child develops over the years between five and thirteen. At present, *Teaching 5–13* comprises three series: **Projects, Reading, Mathematics.**

Projects

Consultant editor: **Frank F. Blackwell**

Each book in this series covers a specific topic and contains a collection of projects relevant to the topic. All the projects are easy to organize. They will appeal to teachers with little experience of project work.

Bakery 356 04883 7   **Giants, witches and dragons** 356 04885 3
Flight 356 04884 5   **North American Indians**   356 04886 1

Reading

Consultant editor: **Donald Moyle**
Principal Lecturer in Education, Edge Hill College of Education and Past-President United Kingdom Reading Association

Though the topic of reading has been split into ten short books, the series has a unity of thinking. They form a compendium of activities, apparatus and games for reading, language development and literature from pre-school to adolescence.

Towards reading	356 05025 4	**Word attack skills**	356 05055 6	**Reading case studies**	356 05059 9
Forthcoming titles		**Beginning to read**	356 05056 4	**Remedial reading**	356 05060 2
Reading teachers' source		**Language at work**	356 05057 2	**Assessing reading progress**	356 05061 0
book	356 05054 8	**Make them think**	356 05058 0	**Using children's literature**	356 05062 9

Mathematics

Consultant editor: **Frank F. Blackwell**
Written by **Malcolm Currie,** Headmaster, Sylvan High School, Croydon, and **Leslie Foster,** Headmaster, Benson Infant and Junior School, Croydon

These books give an overall picture of modern mathematics in the Primary context. The books are based upon the child's developmental stages. So, although it is not possible to use chronological age as the basis of organization, it is useful to indicate an *average* age level for each stage: Book 1, 0–5 years; Book 2, 5–7 years; Book 3, 7–9 years; Book 4, 9–11 years; Books 5 and 6, 11–13 years.

1 Play's the thing	356 05063 7	**4 Physical structures**	356 05066 1
2 Classes and counts	356 05064 5	**5 Symbolic operations: Sets and numbers**	356 05067 X
Forthcoming titles			
3 Sets the scene	356 05065 3	**6 Symbolic operations: Space and quantities**	356 05068 8

Science 5-13 Teachers' Units

Sponsored by The Schools Council, The Nuffield Foundation and The Scottish Education Department

The *Science 5–13* Project has a new and important way of looking at the problem of helping children between the ages of five and thirteen to learn about science. Its trial materials were thoroughly tested in the schools of 27 local education authorities throughout Great Britain.

The principal aim of the teaching ideas and objectives set out in the *Science 5–13* Units is the development in children of an enquiring mind and a scientific approach to problems. The Project recognises that attitudes of enquiry, objective judgement, personal responsibility and ability to work and organize one's work independently can be established in children at an early age.

The books form a series of Units to which teachers can turn for sound advice and guidance, for starting points and background information, when children are working in subject areas covered by the books.

Using the Environment by Margaret Collis

This teachers' compendium of field studies for children aged 5 to 13 completes the *Science 5–13* project. It is divided into four volumes, two of which are further divided in two parts each, giving six books in all. They range from children's first attempts to grasp the numerical and spatial aspects of their outdoor surroundings, whether urban or rural, to their more sophisticated investigations of major biological ideas and relationships using controlled experiments. Equipment and raw materials that children need at all stages of their field studies are covered in detail.